"Quiver of Eros"

By

Nick Anthony Russo

Quiver of Eros – Copyright © 2017

All rights reserved. No part of this publication may be reproduced, stored in a retrieval system, or transmitted in any form or by any means for example, electronic, photocopied, and/or recorded without the prior written permission of the author.

Covers and Edits by iFlow Creative LLC.

I would like to acknowledge the writer that lives inside each and every one of us, for everyone has their own story to tell, and if we are fortunate enough to be able to write it down we may find that it heals us in ways we never imagined possible.

To my most beloved son, Luc-Anthony.

Prologue

My words are my selfies.

Nick Anthony Russo

I.

God moves when we are mysteriously moved.

It's possible in those moments of hungered silence that there comes a knock unexpected upon your door. A knock not patient but a knock not hurried, either. Startled, perhaps even a bit frightened, you might be roused from your respite and if you were, you could very well feel your heart begin to beat a tick faster. Silent and tip-toed, you might slowly inch your way closer towards the door. Once there, you'd might resist the urge to peek through the peephole to see who is outside, because just like a strange delicacy tasted for the first time, you may find it more satisfying to enjoy the flavor of uncertainly than it is to know entirely the composition of what might be waiting on the other side to perhaps consume you first before you could consume it.

Now that the knock has come, you must take a deep breath, you must let caution go, you must fully open the door, and finally, you must let the damned thing inside you....

Nick Anthony Russo

We are not fools. We each know very well the difference
between who kisses us with their lips
and who kisses us with their heart.

We need to be equal in all things between us.
Pulling the weight. Pushing the stars.

But what love didn't ever feel
that way that was thought to be love?
That risk the lone mount, that pain its sole rider.

Quiver of Eros

    I tire of touching things that don't have meaning to me. My next embrace, I am certain, will reach so thoroughly and completely through another person that their ancestors will feel my steely breath upon the napes of their necks. My hands will touch too, and there I will re-write a new history down their spines, and I will traverse their memories with my fingers so far back and beyond to an epoch ancient were language wasn't yet even a mortal tool, just an indistinguishable utterance upon the tongues of those where only fire and a successful hunt mattered and did sustain. And when night does eventually return to its pitchiest black, I'll lie on my back and there, looking straight up, I will hunt and gather the distant stars above me and make a gift to the future generations that will someday too walk Mother Earth.

Nick Anthony Russo

No power on earth can make a woman
do what she doesn't want to do.
But when she so chooses to,
just sit back and get out of the way.

I like you much more
than any other one thing I think about you.

The road to perdition was paved
with the morsels of her desire.
Though her body hungered not any longer,
her spirit still craved the feast of forgiveness.

Although she gave him all she had,
her worth wasn't measured by his leaving,
rather, by the very things that chose to stay.

Quiver of Eros

**Every man whom wages war believes God on his side.
I warrant God should often wonder who is on His.**

Nick Anthony Russo

Quiver of Eros

Love doesn't adhere to a schedule,
so it never may be measured by time
any more than it would ever wait
to indulge your convenience.

I think about you all day.
There is just something about you.
Can't place it.
Don't want to.

**There aren't any coincidences;
there are only circumstances.**

Quiver of Eros

He wasn't perfect.
But he was just perfect enough
to show me that neither was I.
And in this, we each found quiet comfort.

He invaded her body like a rampaging army.
His desire lay siege to her heart,
and there it encamped itself
for the unspoken conflict
that would resume between them.

Time is our most precious commodity.
Living is our most precious luxury.

A feeling like love is best when it lies down
easily and naturally, like moss over a stone.

You can't make magic. Magic just happens.

It was all mistaken. In our pride,
to believe that we can change the temporal world,
all that matters is what waits for us beyond.

I did not know I had a heart.
You filled it with unknown creatures
whose names were joy and hope.
Both sharper blades than any had cut me before.

God sees our little secrets and our little lies.
Moistened lips. Glistened thighs.
Through and through, by and by.

Nick Anthony Russo

New love doesn't come two us quiet and slow.
It comes to us raging like a hurricane
and in its swathe of beauty, old love is swept away.

In truth, we are all players to some degree
until we truly find the one
we wish to give ourselves wholly to.

Lies and deceits remind me of money
and we each know how that can corrupt.
The only currency worth any real value is the truth.

Flattery will get you everywhere,
but so will Uber — and it's probably cheaper.

Quiver of Eros

I really want to wake up next to someone I really want.

Nick Anthony Russo

Quiver of Eros

**Nobody really likes receiving a pep talk.
They always seem pointless
unless you, yourself, are giving one.**

**We are free, but there isn't any real freedom
except the kind that comes with money & power.
If you know any other kind, then run after it.**

**Sometimes we can't get what we need
any more than we can't need what we get.**

We may not have much but we have much of each other.

Quiver of Eros

I will not quarrel with you
because I see your life a quarrel with itself.
When the world has turned, find your true nature.

No one ever stopped her dead in her tracks.
But the footprint he left upon her heart
made forgetting the best part of remembering.

I've loved them. I hated them.
I've drawn them. I released them.
I've found them. I lost them.
I've broken them. I mended them.

Nick Anthony Russo

He lied to me.
I am gone from him
because I don't see his eyes any longer,
just the outline of his body,
and that was never enough.

This dead weight like an anvil upon my chest.
Pressing down on me I grasp for air
just like darkness that seeks lighted closure.

She had crashed and burned many times.
But she never was broken,
and her I.C.U. became a cold realization
of, "I don't need you!"

The arch of her back like the entrance to heaven.
Pearly gates her teeth that, when parted,
spoke only kindly and sounded and formed words
like that of an angel's wings.

**I have been called a hopeless romantic
but in my mind romance is never hopeless.
Just sometimes the people involved in it are.**

Nick Anthony Russo

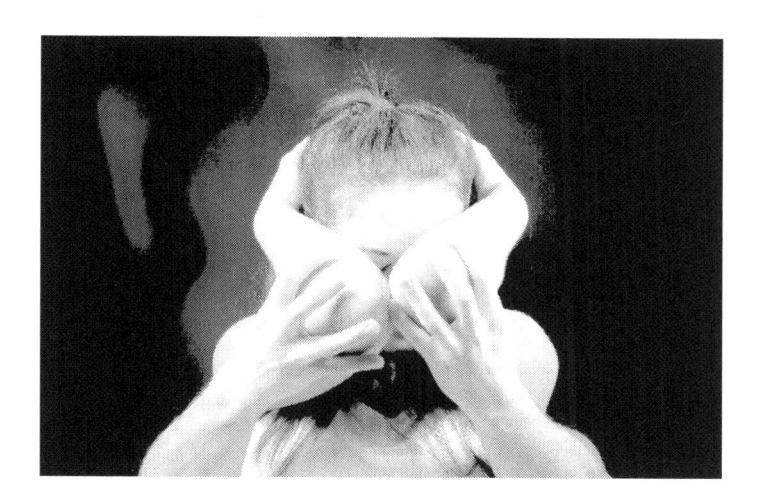

Quiver of Eros

She believed in love at first sight.
Not because she lived "for the moment"
but, rather, because she lived "in the moment."

The most dramatic people I know
live life full of drama.
If they would stop talking but for a moment,
they might have more to say.

No woman's beauty had been more highly praised,
in every key and in every instrument.
No heart she ever stole recovered it.

If he continues to take you for granted,
grant him if he continues,
you won't be his he took for too much longer.

Nick Anthony Russo

**Like a diamond she shone the brightest
when the pressure was greatest.
Flawless of cut, she was a paragon
amongst duller minds.**

Quiver of Eros

**She loved herself
more than any disloyal lover ever could.
Her "ex" never marked her spot
because she never entrusted him her map.**

Nick Anthony Russo

Quiver of Eros

This life made mostly of such beautiful sadness.
And each of us trying desperately
to carve out but the smallest piece of happiness from
it.

Oh yes, they danced as only lovers could.
Rhythm like caged furies between them,
tempered only by wisdom and by a haste vetted.

We don't know what is gone until we have it.

Nobody ever promised you being beautiful
was going to be easy.

**She had been lied to so often
that all men's words seemed but harm.
Today, however, she took in a new scent
and it tasted safe.**

Quiver of Eros

I can't feel anymore,
my hands like gloves turned inside out.
I am outside looking in and I am inside out.
This life, I don't fit.

Some people are so terribly hurt
that they hurt you
before you could ever even think to hurt them.

In our quest for love and to be loved
is in that all the world revolves.
If the earth were flat,
might we circumnavigate it better…?

She enjoyed dancing with the devil
but the only problem
was that she never really knew
when the music had stopped.

Nick Anthony Russo

**Even the patient, mighty oak
owes its majestic life
to the fragile and unassuming acorn...**

**No woman wants to be a Wander Woman.
If you ever have to wander
about what your man is up to,
it might be better to wander away.**

**Imagination is only the vessel.
Words are the liquids that fill it to the top.**

Nick Anthony Russo

She often dreamt of the one that got away.
But, she more happily awoke each morning
next to the one whom never left her side.

A tempest raged inside her,
mixing a cocktail of her emotions
that poured out of her
and into any man that sobered and stilled her.

I like a slow burn.
Something about a meteor that quick sizzles
then fades and doesn't last. I prefer a star.
Sexy is a slow burn.

Nick Anthony Russo

Strong men don't hurt you. Weak men do.

Quiver of Eros

**In a world of instant gratification,
she took more time to truly know herself
than she did trying to forget herself.**

**The thing I appreciate the most about lies,
innuendo and rumors
is that they are just that.**

**The deepest of our intimacies
is never the co-joining of the hips.
They are only of eye to eye,
of hand to hand and of lip to lip.**

Nick Anthony Russo

**Their love betrayed all sin
and made even loss feel claustrophobic.
To say they loved one another deeply
was a lie falsely told.**

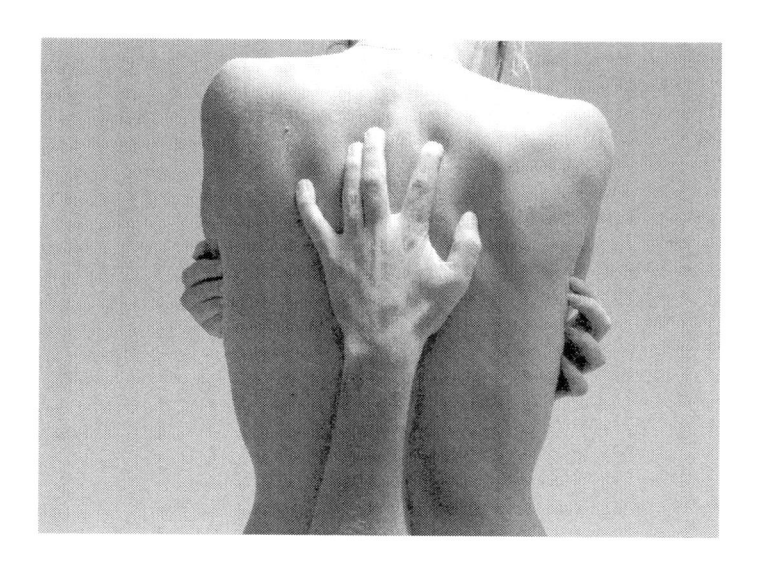

It's ok to let him know. But once he does,
then it's his turn to reciprocate or not.
If he truly wants you, he'll show you.

Of course I could feel all of her weight
when she pressed down upon me.
She was thick with thought
and she was heavy with emotion.

The thing we hate the most in people is very usually
the thing we hate the most about ourselves.

I get it. You are scared.
You don't want me to get too excited about you
because you don't want you to get too excited
about me.

I imagine what heaven must be like:
Going back to your beginning,
correcting all your mistakes
and just loving and being loved.

Quiver of Eros

**Little things always constitute
the content of larger things.
That's why the details matter in love.**

Nick Anthony Russo

Quiver of Eros

**I met a woman today.
She asked me if I was moving?
I said, yes. She then asked, where to?
I replied, heaven.**

**Your journey is etched in your skin
either by scar or ink. Each drew blood.
Each tells a story. Each a reminder. Expression heals.**

Nick Anthony Russo

All she owned were her skin and her bones.
All she wanted was his flesh and his spirit.

Inside. It was in that moment that I stopped to hate.
Not that I wanted to but, rather, because I could.
Outside.

I like the way you like me.
But I'd love the way you'd love me even better.

Even the greatest of mysteries can fade from us
if we don't water and feed them just enough
for them to remain faithful to us.

Quiver of Eros

**If you really love someone
you'd run through a brick wall to be with them.
No excuse.**

**Of course she laughed at fools.
She was ruler of kings
and she taught wisemen their truths.
Yes, God had a daughter too.**

Nick Anthony Russo

**She was a woman beyond her time.
When the world thought to silence or disavow her,
she loved louder and let go even tighter.**

The tears that roll the slowest down our face
are usually the ones
that have held in the most pain and suffering.

There is always a beginning to the end.
And there is always an end to the beginning.

**Having fun makes you forget.
Being happy makes you remember.
Feeling content makes you do both at the same time
by being present.**

I spoke to an Atheist the other day.
She spoke of her belief of only fact.
I spoke back to her that my belief was my fact.

Have you ever felt alone
then you weren't alone
but you preferred being alone?

Nick Anthony Russo

**Never let anyone set your mood.
That's the point. Just serve with love.
The match is best played with the least unforced
errors.**

**Close your eyes. Look skyward.
Breathe. Then just let go.
He said that it was o.k.**

**Simplicity:
Men want to be needed.
Women want to be loved.**

Nick Anthony Russo

Quiver of Eros

At the edge of your mind is a forest
where poachers think to steal your growth.
No game, warden, trust your instincts.

Can you imagine right next to you
a person seeking what you seek?
Be kind, we are all so very much the same.

We only truly discover how fragile we are
when we are made to realize
how strong we've had to become.

The most gorgeous of God's creations
are often the most fragile.
Never confuse beauty with invulnerability.

Nick Anthony Russo

Beauty without charm is just vanity.

**Move on to somebody
who can't stand not seeing you.**

**We grow the most when we suffer;
we live the most when we love.**

What is a crush but a tiger in a cage yet unreleased...

So I sit still. I'll let God be my motion.

**When we are able to openly talk about it,
we are likely getting better about it.**

Nick Anthony Russo

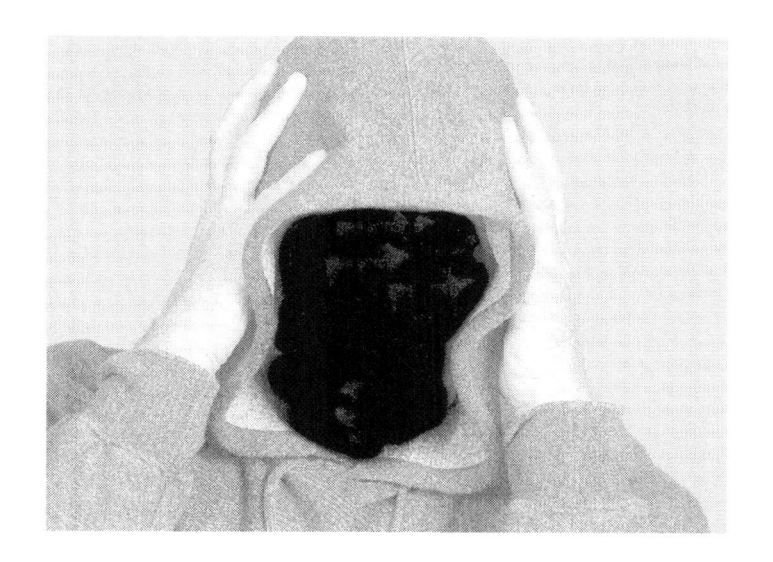

Quiver of Eros

**If you should ever feel hate in your heart,
let it only be your rudder but never your anchor.**

**Have you ever not known where you were going
only to wind up exactly where you needed to be?**

Nick Anthony Russo

**When I awoke up this morning,
I saw a new day dawning.
That's because the sun tasted the moon
and warmly kissed her a goodnight.**

**I am not looking for a big ego.
I am looking for a big heart.**

**I am looking for that one woman
I think of as out of my league
just as she thinks I am out of hers.**

She knew she was a disaster waiting to happen.
But she also knew her rescue crew
was her own abilities and her own determination.

I would prefer to be alone
than ever to be discontented.
I didn't say unhappy. I said discontented.
There is a difference.

If I should fall fast, just know that I love hard.

No one who protects their heart fully
is able to love fully.
Just let go.

**Her name was truth.
She was all the things people thought
but were too afraid to say.**

**People that really want, want.
So, say it less. Mean it more.**

**I am a ghost not even capable
of haunting my own body.**

Quiver of Eros

**When you are deeply in love,
the world does indeed conform to your own blissful imaginings
and then, magically, transmutes itself yet again,
into an unfolding of infinite possibilities....**

Nick Anthony Russo

We all long to be somewhere different
when we are not in love.
When we are in love with someone, though,
any place together is paradise...

Sometimes the only place we truly belong
is the only place we never allow ourselves ever to
go...

Love those back fiercely who love you
for one day THAT day may never be the same...

Nick Anthony Russo

**Much of what we call progress
is simply been a matter of remembering
what was once forgotten.**

We truly understand death for the first time
when we place our hands upon whom we love.

When love between two people is right, it's easy.

Broken hearts don't ever fully heal,
they just re-shape themselves into smaller pieces
with bigger hopes towards a better future.

Nick Anthony Russo

**What you seek
is usually greater than what you'll find.**

Quiver of Eros

**It's always changing
in who we are supposed to love
and who we are not.
The only thing that stays the same
is that we want who we want.**

Nick Anthony Russo

Quiver of Eros

**You can sometimes better judge
a man's values and integrity
more by what he does after his marriage
than during his marriage.**

**Intimacy is the real magic.
The woman sawed in half is just sex.**

Nick Anthony Russo

It's not always possible to get the answers we need.
Sometimes a person's actions have to be enough
for us just to move on.

When we are forced to stop loving a person,
we always must re-learn how to love ourselves again.

It so easy to become victimized
by our own tragic story
that we often forget that we
are the strongest part of the narrative.

**If I ever get back to where I used to be,
I can promise you I will never go back to who I was.**

Nick Anthony Russo

Quiver of Eros

She wasn't a wreck.
She was just a fender bender
who crashed into the truth much more bravely
than she ever swerved into condoning a lie.

The truth doesn't belong to any of us.
But it is always owed to the person you love.

We'll watch the stars burnout the night
'til the morning skies.
There I'll make all your pain and grief my own
and wear it in disguise.

Nick Anthony Russo

Your words don't hurt me, but your silence does. And just so you know, loving you was far easier than liking you ever was.

Quiver of Eros

All your empty promises
I've redacted from my memory.
The storybook that was once us
is now just blank pages bound by nothingness.

Just because you two clicked
doesn't mean he or she isn't still swiping right.
Intuition is soft. Desire is loud.
Trust the frequency.

Dating. Where you just get tired of dressing up
and telling your story again.

**I am many things to many people.
But what matters most is what I am to myself.**

Quiver of Eros

II.

What if we just stopped? I forgave someone today. I did it for them. That I didn't do it for me might sound to you cavalier, brash even - it's not, though. They suffered because of the anguish they caused me. They saw this tragedy within me. A total wreck I am, not just a fender-bender. They felt the pain that crashed and wailed up inside me, that burst into reply through worded anger! The type of vitriol only a deeply afflicted heart could render, that lashed back at them with stain and permanence.

My poison administered: it took its intended effect. Sick, they re-read the words they wrote to me. They must have considered themselves deeply and did know, then, themselves a casualty of their own making. To muster. To arms. Bravely and thoughtfully, with remorse, they offered apology. The apology was sincere, noble even. I let time pass in its way, as it always does, and in deep thought, I wrote back simply that, "All is forgiven." Then, I was soothingly reminded of the liturgy of the Catholic priest. The scripture of words that reads: THAT TOO SHALL PASS....

I knew then, as I know now, those words were not meant only for our comforted miseries, but also for us in our fleeting joys. All things are temporal.

Nick Anthony Russo

What if we just stopped?

Could the meaning of life be the fearing of death? Could the fear of death be the meaning of life? Or is it the many, many things in between them that constitute the gap between our living and our dying? Have you ever been walking or driving home on auto-pilot and then, suddenly, you just become aware of yourself? It's a strange feeling, comparable only to waking up from a dream, and it's ironic in that it is in direct juxtaposition to our subconscious. You might begin to feel warm and tingly all over. You momentarily might lose purchase of yourself and your perspective of the world might appear a bit off. During this peculiar self-realization there couldn't be more than a few uncomfortable seconds that passes by, but your world appears to be hurling toward you, yet in the slowest possible motion. Anxiously, you look down at your feet hoping to get your bearings, or you grip tighter upon the steering wheel for something solid and reassuring to hang onto. You know it well: that physical touch that you instinctively search and long for that keeps you grounded and in touch with reality. If this is true for each of us and to any degree, are we therefore not designed to be alone? Does being with another person make us less aware of ourselves, and in so doing, less aware of all that plagues this Earth and its people? It must be so because we always reflect the most when we our alone and isolated. It's an immutable fact that we do, but it truly so confounding to me.

Is it joy about forgetting or about remembering, maybe both? Are we joyful that we have fond memories of what is lost to us, but at the same time without joy because they are gone? How do we go about reconciling the two? Can they be reconciled, or are they designed not to be?

I have so many questions, but I am not looking for any answers - the answers lead to just more questions and the questions just lead to less answers. So I sit. So I wait. Lonely, isolated but aware. And then it occurs to me: God places people in our lives to forget the horrors of this world, but He would sooner take them away, despite our coupling, should we ever forget our responsibility and should we ever not assist those less fortunate than ourselves.

One arrow is very easily broken. The binding of two or more together, always the more difficult to break. Aim for love.

Just love.

There are many forms of cruelty but some are more harmful than others. Personally, when I was younger and less aware of my own shortcomings, I was guilty of what I am about to share with you, regrettably more so than most. I used my words, both written and verbally, as weapons and my target was typically not as well-versed nor prepared for this type assault in what I would call the "black art". I say "art" because it takes a vivid imagination, as well as a baseline of background information about someone to deeply hurt them with your words. And I say "black" because it is the intimate knowledge that we gain from someone opening up to us, and violating that trust to strike or retaliate against them is one of the most reprehensible things we could ever do to one another! And, as I have already made admittance to before, dear readers, I have in my past been guilty of such vile and base neglect. Furthermore, I say to you without the slightest bit of reservation, It is not something I am proud of in the least.

Today, however, I am more careful with my words but, unfortunately, some people we know either personally or impersonally, may not be. Which brings me to the point of my post: demand of yourself to be most careful and most judicious with any personal pain or broken hearted testimony people share with you. Never, I say never, retaliate against them about their personal tragedies even if you are scorned, betrayed, devalued or otherwise put to poor use by them.

It is the Devil in our mind that makes us become too badly hurt and too gravely wounded without the ability to temper it with a sense of calm understanding and with quiet humility. Also, we should know full well that it is the Devil that lives better and further away from God when he has both possession of your heart and when he has his vengeance through you....

Let God and Christ be your guide and try and come to better terms with the realization that our anger and our vindication is most human - there is no getting around that inherent trait in any of us...Lastly, I urge you to remember this: the nobler and the more spiritual the path is to strongly resist and mindfully tread not where the Devil does. By so doing, we can become more like our Father and more like His Son.

When she arched her back and stretched like a cat, I knew what was on her mind. Desire clawed out from her pores and a soft, sensual moan smoldered forth from her loins. She ached and softly purred in ways only she could when the man she was with made her feel most safe and gave her the elevated place beside him where she belonged.

She surrendered the most tender parts of herself to him and held herself accountable. To blame her lust on another, she knew, was foolish and gave her false shelter. It slowly, but surely, weakened her resolve in all the other aspects of her life. Armed thus, she was determined not to be taken advantage of nor to take advantage of someone else. Rather, she promised herself when she did give her womanhood to a man, it would only be on the condition of exclusivity between them. She knew that this union was no guarantee of a long term partnership, but her conscience was more at ease and she was better able to pursue freely the things she thought worthy of herself. She never chastised herself again after this self-revelation as she made it a point to be most conscientious; not just when it came to lust, but also when it came to love. She did this because she knew the line between them can sometimes become blurred, and blinded by it was the last thing she ever

wanted to be.

Do you not see me any longer? I walk the same hallways as you and I wonder, when you do, what colors you see there upon them? I see pale, lifeless shades but I don't recall them ever being that way before. I went into the bedroom, the one we never use. I see baby blue painted on the walls and I ask myself why we never changed the color? The small person that once lived there is gone and baby blue is not his color any longer. I believe he outgrew it long ago, but it appears neither of us did. It's sad in its way, but I am smart enough to realize very few things I can expect to stay the same, especially people.

It's quiet here, now. I love it, and at the same time I hate it. The only noise I do hear from time to time is you moving upstairs, the way you try and quietly slide your feet across the wooden floors as to make the least amount of noise possible. It is so loud to me in those moments, like a herd of rumbling buffalo that tear into my eardrums. I know it is not the sound you make that bothers me but, rather, it is the person who makes the sound that troubles me. Are these the small, insignificant things that signal to us that our love HAS run its course? I believe that they are and I ask myself why DID I stay?

Do you not see me any longer? I walk the same

hallways as you and I wonder when you do, what colors do you see there upon them? I see pale, lifeless shades but I don't recall them ever being that way before. I walk upstairs to see you and you turn around to look back at me but you don't look at me with your heart anymore, just your eyes. I know this is how I must look to you because love, or the lack of love, is always a reflection of whom we are with.

The furniture in our bedroom is just that: furniture. The bed, especially, used to be a place where our love was strongest and made manifest. Where each our hopes and dreams took seed, gave birth, then took flight. I don't hate you. I hate myself, though, for not having the courage to break my own heart. Sounds foolish to say and to hear but when you really think about it, there is truth in my words. You begin to walk past me and toward the stairs. Your shoulder brushes up against mine and as you do, I feel the slightest bit of energy pass between us. Are these the small, insignificant things that signal to us that our love HAS NOT run its course? I believe that they are and I ask myself why DIDN'T I stay?

Quiver of Eros

Do you know that small voice, that voice inside your head? That one we each have, the one that sometimes compels us to say mean and even scandalous things on social media about others whether we know them personally or not. You know precisely well: the type of words that aren't very nice...the kind of words that you could easily of stopped yourself from saying, but you say them anyway. Where does that come from? Are we angry? Are we jealous? Is there something to be gained that we aren't privy to? Does it please us to lash out or to re-direct our hostilities toward the blameless and the innocent and in doing so, does this bring us some measure of self-satisfaction? I catch myself sometimes...near the keyboard, mouse in hand, my thoughts twisted and contorted in their vicious way where the pen (so to speak) is, indeed, mightier than the sword. What pound of flesh do or did I take...do or did you take? Do we so easily and without remorse carve up one another like prime rib on a skewer just to be served up warmly for the benefit of so many purveyors of our contemptuous words? Does this validate us? I wonder and that I wonder and in wondering, I wonder what explanation could there be?

We each stop and look at the car wreck. We

know this about ourselves: we will look. I look. We can't turn away from neither death nor injury—we are too much fascinated by the suffering of others because we know full well our own. This instinct doesn't make us not human, nay. Rather, I believe it is the very thing that makes us human! Evolution of our species, the necessity of "flight or fight" when judging potential threats to us that is the predicator built into the very fiber of our DNA...a civilized collective we consider ourselves and IF we truly and reasonably are, where do we draw the line with our baseless criticisms of others? What imaginary line in the sand must be crossed for us to become cognizant that, ultimately, our wayward words do more damage to ourselves than they do to others?

Next time you type. Next time I type. Give pause. Think. Consider. Who do I want to hurt today? Or, who would I rather to make feel good today?

Now: Free yourself from yourself.

Her heart had been cheated. Her teeth had been stained. Her lips had been sealed. Her mind had been deadened. Her hands had been emptied. Her eyes had been closed. Her hair had been damaged. Her gait had been abbreviated. Her emotions had been edited. Her posture had been realigned.

Oh yes, through the years she is much different now but who among us is not? She could remember very little of her past and she didn't particularly want nor care to reflect upon those vague, painful memories anyhow. Today, instead, she is more certain and more contented with her future. She is not a seer, not a jinn, not a prophetess nor any such an arcane being. She is a just a woman possessed with the gift of intuition just like each of her other worldly sisters. When she uses her formidable power, she is undaunted and fearless, and she easily unmasks those that would conceal themselves from her as she is able to discern their truths just as readily as does she uncover their lies. But this knowledge does not please her nor make her feel ascendant nor impervious to the discovery—oh no, it pulls at her and weighs her down, but burdened thus, she is no less strong. She finds a sort of peace within this strength because she sees far beyond herself which grants her grace which, in turn, gives her a quiet, soft humility. She may indeed be broken, but she is far from alone and in this fellowship, she is most intact.

And there she stood in the center of a violent coliseum of her own making. Gladioli, tridents, and bucklers of her deceased foes shined steely and dangerous in the sun as they littered the blood-soaked sand. The slain and disemboweled bodies no longer companioned their weapons as one by one they were hauled off in a singular heap or by an individual part that once had summed them wholly. The iron gates began to screech and whine as they were pulled open by rusted chains that held the slave as sure as it did the metallic barrier that groaned upward with beast-like contempt. Once fully drawn up, out came a hyena, an elephant, a wild boar, a buffalo, a bear, a lion, a tiger, a bull, a wolf, and a leopard. Each carnivore encircled and hungrily advanced upon her position with no thought of the their own natural enmity toward one another, and she made small, concentrated circular movements as if to counter each successive threat which she knew doing was next to impossible. She was unarmed and unshielded, but her eyes cast daggers and her lips snarled in resolute defiance. Armed thus, she began to pray for the strength and the endurance to defeat these deadly threats that were just about to strike at her. With great urgency, she spoke and cast out loud a prayer that labeled each animal by its name—and, as she did, one by one, they each began to cower away and retreat back into their iron den.

From there they were replaced by a singular, smaller and more timid animal: a lamb. As the lamb cautiously made its way toward her outstretched arms, it bleated out its natural call and when it did it sounded to her just like milk and just like honey. This soothing sound immediately caused her to crumble to her knees and with what remaining strength she had left, she allowed her tears to fall greedily down her face. She had not cried in years and this battle and this struggle was all she had come to know. But on this day, this very blessed day, the body of Christ did mark and did relieve her of each her sufferings and the lamb took her away where others could not but hope to follow.

Quiver of Eros

Who will have your heart again? No-one will. Why won't anyone ever have it? Because it's gone. Where did it go to? It left with another. Do you think you can get it back? Do we ever get time back? No, I suppose not but we both agreed that I was to ask the questions and you were to just answer them. That wasn't a question. But I had to let you know that we had gotten off track in our interview. That wasn't a question, either. Fair enough. Ah, you did it again! Oh, I believe I see where this headed and I will make certain I am more careful with you in the future by constructing each of my statements as a question: what do you think about that? I think you are catching on.

Good, may we start over? We can try to. I would like it very much if you would just indulge me a moment longer: will you? Yes, I will do my best. How do you feel without a heart? Alone, afraid, anxious, lifeless, dark, ugly, numb, fat, thin, starved, bloated, nauseous, searching, floating, hopelessness and a sense of never-ending. If love were to come and try to mend your heart again, would you even recognize it for what it is? I doubt it. Why not? I think because when you've been in the dark for so long it becomes your only trusted, faithful companion. You begin to build a certain bond, an unbreakable partnership that you come to depend upon entirely and there is a type of comfort in this. So, in short, you are saying that you learn to adapt to your forlorn situation and this becomes your new reality? Yes, something like this.

Then, with all hope and promise gone and no heart to give, what do you live for? I don't really know the answer to that question. Would you like for me to take you away from here? Yes. Do you care where we go? No. Can you close your eyes? Yes. Can you stop to breathe while your eyes are closed? For a minute, perhaps. With your eyes closed and while holding your breath, do you hear something? I do. What do you hear? A beating. Does it sound like a heart? Yes. Can you tell me whose heart it is? No. Do you think it is your heart beating? No, I can't really tell but I do hear a beating. Well, it is a heart, it's just not your heart that you hear: it is mine. Hey, that wasn't a question! I know, but it is THE ANSWER. Who are you, anyway? I am the one that will share my heart with you. Hey, that wasn't a question, either. I know, but it is THE ANSWER.

May I ask you a few more questions? Yes. Do you believe in God? Yes, I do. Why do you believe in God? Because I chose to. Can you see God? No, but all around me I see His faithful works: animals, flowers, mountains, rivers, oceans, stars, clouds, the sun, the moon.

Do you think that in believing in something you can't see is called faith? I do. Can you see your heart? No. Do you think it's inside you beating away? I do. Why? Because I am here speaking with you and if I didn't have a heart my blood would never reach my vital organs and I would be dead. So, now you choose to believe you have a heart? Yes, in a manner of speaking but only for myself and not enough to give away to someone else. Isn't that selfish? Maybe, but what I have left I am very much in need of. Do you recall that I gave you my heart? I did hear you say those words, yes. Do you know why I gave my heart to you? No, I don't. Because, like yourself, I have faith in the Lord and also like you, I choose to believe. You made a mistake again: that was a statement and not a question.

I know, but it is THE ANSWER.

Nick Anthony Russo

Life is gone in less than a whisper. Whose parting words that none but angels hear. Blessed are those that are left behind. One day for us, another day as more near.

Quiver of Eros

There is just something about you. Why is it, do I think I could love you so much? I think it might in the way you like me: the way you look at me, the way sometimes, ironically, you can't look at me at all because it might reveal too much of your heart to me—but, avoiding eye contact with me tells me all I need to know. If you are scared to love believe me, I am too. It's not my fear of suffering, oh no, it's the fear I may disappoint you and in so doing, disappoint myself. I haven't much to give because I feel all dried up. I've lost so many things dear to me and it has taken a heavy toll. When things we lose or die that we cherish, they take a bit of you with them. When pieces of yourself are gone this changes your composition. We are not more for our suffering but less. Not less better. Not less hopeful. Not less loving. It's just that we have less to share of ourselves and it simply cannot be helped-it is just the way of things. I love you no less, I just have less to love you with.

We don't own people, we only own ourselves
and even then just fragments at best, because
sometimes our mind has, well, a mind of its own.
Buddha teaches that all attachment to others will
always be self-imbued with suffering. He is correct,
in my humble estimation. But, what of attachment to
ourselves? Can there be parts we can completely
release that are the very definition of who we are,
either directly or indirectly? Can our subconscious,
which is master of so much of our thought, behavior
and action, ever be disassociated from our
consciousness so that we may become truly
enlightened? And by enlightened, I don't mean
solvent in our knowledge nor accredited in our
wisdom but, rather, enlightened in such a way that
we know full well our own failings and
imperfections, therefore, we must be tolerant of
ourselves just as much as to others, if not even more
so.

I know what love is. Yes, you do for a certainty because when you love someone or something, it invariably hurts. But why must it hurt to know that you love? Well, have you ever loved and it not hurt?

Yes, I believe that I have. Really? How did it not hurt? Well, I only felt this immense attraction and I couldn't keep my hands off him and we had so many things in common and everything between us was just easy—we seemed to flow in all things and always in the same direction. Wouldn't that make it love? Yes, it would. But let me ask you another question, a more exacting one. Yes? Are you still together with this person? No, I am not. Why did you two part ways? Because I met someone else who I am actually more attracted to and he makes me laugh until I literally cry. Interesting. And, do you miss this other person that you once felt love for? Not at all! And you feel nothing for him now—no pain, no regret, no anguish? Not a one! Have you seen this person out with another woman? Yes. And how did that make you feel? I couldn't have cared less! Then I put this to you: you were not in love. That was just your ideal of love. That was lust, an attraction, a calibrated harmony of two physical beings that confused love with a more base desire which lead you to confuse the emotions. It is common enough and I don't ridicule you for your mistake. We've all made it-in fact, it is a necessary component to distinguish between lust and love. I see your point. Do you? I think I do. Okay, let's do a simple thing to test my theory, okay? Sure. This new more attractive, funnier person, are you still together? Yes. Do you love him? Yes, very much. Why? Because I don't see him as much as I did the other guy and I miss him like crazy! Why do you not see him as much? Well, I am embarrassed to admit it but he is married. Ah, I see. Does it hurt? Yes it does, very much. Why does it hurt? Because he told me he would never leave his wife, but that he loves me. Then I put this to you: you were not in love. That was just your ideal of love. That was a lust, an attraction, a calibrated harmony of two physical beings that confused love with a more base desire which lead you to confuse the emotions. Then please help me to define love, Father?!

Listen and I will.

Love is thus: your body will pulsate with an indescribable energy. Your love will be available to you entirely and not even remotely beholden to someone else. All things you see will appear different, better, brighter, softer, less harsh. You will feel stronger and have a greater pity towards the

disenfranchised and the poverty-stricken. You will want to just blend in with your love, and camouflage yourself from the world on most days. You will be more patient. You will listen more, and talk less. You will see the injustices of a world gone awry and your empathy will be most overwhelming. You will want to mend broken relationships. You will want to renew old ones. And all these things are beautiful and so welcome in your life! But, be very aware, each have their cost, for none are meant to last or, at least, last in the way you view and perceive time. I, your Father, blink and a century passes by. You blink and but a second is gone. Life here on this planet is perishable. There is a shelf-life and the products of each our lives have expiration dates, most especially true love. Before you think I am cruel, consider this: even if you truly love a man as I have described above until the end and until you meet death, the either of you, there is still going to be pain associated to that passing. The two, both the pain and the love, are intrinsically bound to one another. There is no way to circumvent them, they can never be sundered and there is no way to not have one without having the other. So, rejoice and understand their union and accept that inevitability. Knowing this will bring you love. Knowing this will bring you

peace.

Quiver of Eros

All the same...in the end, we are all the same. No color, no creed, no race may differ us...the world we inhabit is primarily constructed of pain, the grey architecture is angled and curved and even misshapen, the most visible commonality is of strife and of struggle, where the each of us try so desperately to carve out but a niche of personal happiness and but a particle of hopeful respite. We are all brothers and sisters of gloom, and this bond is made more salient by the way in which the each of us claws and scratches and maims one another for a promise that never can be quite fulfilled. A promise heard on the wind or in a dream, where others we know, or don't know, may claim them as their own and in their possession doth make it appear more real to us than not and, in such lasting effect, does envy further taint and disillusion us, our suffering soul...Where one thing is not enough so two things are needed more, but then the two is gained and even that not enough, so four is needed that much more...and on and on and on and so on it goes...We are not happy nor are we hardly even close to content and, in the end, we are each so truly the same as again no color, no creed, no race may differ us. A circular rock, wrought of pain and gross negligence is our worldly inheritance and, brothers and sisters, we are each the beneficiaries that, if we were ever really given a choice, we would much prefer never to have to make claim.

The only real valuable currency in this world is truth or, at least, the truth we choose to make self-admission to. While it not a lie that we each have a varying degree of skeletons in our closet, there is a deeper truth within us that we each have a very difficult time of admitting even to ourselves. A truth so dark and so deep that we must try and block it out of our mind entirely like it never existed in the first place and then, fold it safely away in the back drawers of our subconscious and there, keep it remained and undiscoverable by even our closest of intimates for what we hope all eternity...

And neither her bravery nor her conviction were stunted nor altered by what others might of thought of her but, rather, they were each made most inviolate, for she was a woman that wore her truth as she did a crown and her bearing resembled a scepter for majestically and unashamedly did she carry herself...

Many a potential relationships have been made to seem undesirable and even deemed ruinous by envious persons that would whisper false and damaging accusations into your ear about the ones that you would of have liked to have known better beforehand. Sometimes it's more advantageous for one to step off the cliff of discovery yourself than it is to stay firmly grounded next to a "friend" that covetously wishes you to themselves.

Nick Anthony Russo

I remember a time when we hated calculus instead of our neighbor. I remember getting a call on the house phone from a girlfriend which made me more joyous than a text from one by mobile phone today. I remember throwing the football on concrete streets with friends instead of throwing rocks at our police. I remember that if the gym coach gave you a swat, you damn well had it coming and you didn't get the right to sue neither him nor the school. I remember saying a pledge each morning that provided routine, endowed calm reassurance, and gave me pause for a moment to think of nothing else but what I said although I didn't necessarily know what it meant. I remember scores were settled by the bike rack with fists and we chased by foot the girls we liked to show our adolescent interest. We held open doors. We said 'yes, ma'am' and 'no, sir' and the quickest way to a "time out" wasn't on a basketball court or a football field, but by coming home past the hour expected by our bosses, our parents. I remember the simple things back then compared to a world today that is full of complexity and too much choice. We used to be a simple people and by simple I don't mean ignorant or easily impressed. We were satisfied in ways we can't be today because we are constantly bombarded with faster and newer information and transfixed by artificially enhanced images that make us value less what we have next to us already and, worse, makes us question our own self-worth. I remember those days. And those days remember me. K.I.S.S.

Did you miss me while you were looking for yourself? Did you think you'd ever wake up alone from the dream we had built? Did you think our song would ever make you cry because it sounded different without me? Did you think your courage would forsake you when you tried to go inside the places we used to visit together? Did you ever imagine a road, a sign, or building could be so deserted when you alone travelled upon it, past it, or near it? Did you know the wind would blow differently, that the sun would shine less warm, and that the stars would not be as bright? Did your food not taste as good, did the wine make you not remember to forget, and did the dessert not taste as sweet?

Did you realize what you had, had you as much as you had yourself? Did you imagine that my smell could not be conjured up at your whim? Did you know my fingers would leave prints own your soul? Did you know my voice could be heard in any tongue? Did you know we now pray for different things? Did you know our God was always the same?

Did you know our last kiss, did you know our last embrace, and did you know those were the last of each of them?

Would you of stopped time? Would time have stopped you?

There is no such thing as truly living in the present because everything we see still takes a millisecond for our brain to register and, in that slight lag, does time become but a memory.

So take heart, lost love, we each live life but a fraction in the past.

And just like she was gone. Like a lit cigar whose ashes had been tapped, she fell into the ocean where her fire had been snuffed out and with it, too, her vague memory was buried from me like some padded treasure chest that had sunk to the bottom of the same sea, whose contents seemed much more valuable simply because I didn't know what secrets or valuables she possessed for she kept them hidden from me, but not out of simple greed, but out of a darker fear which she held in check closely to her own heart, maintained safely there and locked away deep, deep inside.

There are two sides to everyone. Therefore, it imperative to be with a person that brings out the best and not the worst of you.

That is the real question we must each ask ourselves: do we stay with our partner because it familiar even in its pain or, do we leave because we each know that it far better and healthier for us to do so? The answer never easy and to action, even harder. But these false bonds that bind are but illusions we tell ourselves to bring comfort and justification to staying even when we are fully aware that the relationship has run its course. The truth a hard thing, but in its hardness we find ourselves truncated to the barest of elements and distilled to the most basic of reductions—a free form able to recapture what we once were and what we still plan on being when we choose simply to let go...

It is often said that God does not give us more than we can handle. I have often thought and carefully considered this universal Christian saying and belief and, of late, I have come to a very different conclusion: I believe God does indeed GIVE US MORE THAN WE CAN HANDLE for the very reason that we will know Him, need Him, speak to Him, and rely on Him even more.

"I love you." Ever have there been more powerful words? These words have launched ships. These words have captured our imagination. These words have enslaved our soul. These words have helped us fend off and to better battle our own fears. These words have surrendered our more base human emotions. These words have indentured our servitude. These words have lifted us above and beyond the ramparts of our own limitations. And these words have fought many a war to see us the victor upon the battlefield, where death or loss may eventually precede and indeed consume us, but the memory itself sustains life even when the heart can but beat no more.

Heaven is where you are completely reunited with all the things you've ever lost: Your keys. Your dog. Those earrings. Your mind. Your soul. That sibling. Your drive. That money. That friend. Your heart. Your time. That Summer. Your self. Your purse. That smell. Your wallet. Your dad. Your belief. Those pants. Your voice. That touch. Your way. That love. Your mom. Those memories. Your magic. That joy. Your reason. That race. Your touch. Your grandparent. That fight. That game. Those glasses. That hope...And that which we once were or might have ever of hoped to have been...

Quiver of Eros

Nick Anthony Russo

Excerpts

I've become so numb to the pain. Every single day...each day like the one before it and each day thereafter, the exact same...a kaleidoscope of sameness reflected upon every single thing I see, turned not to vivid color but to a lifeless palette of black and white set upon a canvas of incessantly moving parts, populated by faceless people who go about their day returning to homes or streets diseased with immoral deed and carnal thought.

Waxed stick figures we've become: stretched to our limits, bent to the will of people even more corrupt than ourselves, emaciated from enlightened thought and starved for purpose in a world that glorifies riches and beauty beyond graceful humility and the composition of one's character.

A vigilante is needed to cleanse and debunk this myth we call wealth and happiness. A sole purveyor of death that would rather take risk and assume adventure than to stagnant in a cesspool of self-delusion.

A creature of the night that doesn't stalk its prey, but, rather lures them in with the promise of sex and of sweet release.

I would own the streets this night and, if there is

a God, let him show his face soon because if he doesn't, then the devil may very well write a book of his own.

That is why you always text me so late at night with either whiskey or wine on your mind and just sex on your breath.

With that we would both laugh uncontrollably and she would not be able to help herself and snort out loud, which would only cause us to laugh longer and still more until neither of us could catch our breath! When we did finally stop, we would both just lie there on our backs and look up at the ceiling. Where I saw only darkness and infinity, I imagined she saw light and some kind of absolutism.

She had a life to return to, a husband and one son. I had no one and my family consisted of long lost memories and faded, parched dreams. Where she had an oasis, I had but a mirage.

This was when she was the sweetest and kindest and she would try and comfort me, and I was grateful because I knew she meant every word of it, "Liz, we are both lonely. We both long for contented hearts. But don't rush to judgement and think I am better off than you. Just ask yourself this, and be honest with yourself—is it better to be lonely by yourself or, is it better to be lonely with someone your stuck with but don't love?"

I didn't answer and she didn't press me for one. She quickly got up from the bed, took out a brush from her purse, and combed her hair.

Then she put her expensive clothes and shoes on, straightened up her posture, placed eight $100 bills on one of my two nightstands and walked out the front door with not so much as a backwards glance.

My Love Life,

Sometimes people come into our lives to change our trajectory.

That it is why I don't believe in coincidences, and that I only believe

in circumstances.

I hope you are not being too hard on yourself and I more sincerely

hope you begin again to live life in the present. The past is a very

harsh mistress and she wants nothing more than to have you all to

herself. But she is only capable of loving in the worst types of ways

because she knows there is another beyond her and this doesn't sit

well, so she desperately clings to you and if you aren't strong and

courageous enough, you'll never be able to break free of her.

Love, Mom

This was the last letter my mother ever wrote to me. I always kept it with me and I treasured it beyond all things, especially since it somehow magically retained on its singular, yellowed page the lavender smell my mother scented herself with just before she went out with one of her paramours. As I carefully folded it up and placed it back neatly into the drawer of my nightstand, I looked back over my shoulder and glanced tenderly at the long blonde hair that spilled out from the covers next to me. As I gently moved closer to her body, I could better smell the remnants of last night's pleasures: the delicate bouquet of wine we drank intermingled with the softest hint of her intoxicating perfume, but, mostly what I took in, was the rarest of spices and the most alluring decadence of her womanhood that re-aroused me most immediately!

I must have moved too quickly or too strongly toward her because the spell was broken and, in that precise moment, she turned back to look into my eyes and beckoned sleepily, "Please, Elizabeth, go back to bed. You know I have to leave soon and sleeping next to you is where I always rest my best."

With that she turned back around and became

very quiet as I could hardly even hear her breathe. I badly needed my own rest, so I moved closer still to her, put my form behind her form, gently cupped her breasts, and tender sleep found me quickly once again.

Nick Anthony Russo

He had lied and disappointed me so often that when I watched his tongue move, it flickered in and out of his mouth like that of a snake. So far removed was I from feeling anything for him, my heart felt like a missing limb—a phantom limb that couldn't pick up and put back together our past, nor one that could construct a future where all hope and promise had been severed because this man could not be to true to any one women. But that wasn't the most painful part for me, oh no! It was something different—so far different that the description escaped me more, I think, out of self-preservation than from the lack of some reassuring adjective we each tell ourselves to make our pain seem manageable and even surmountable. I haven't some profound, enlightened answer for you because, as you well know yourself, the heart is never connected to the mind: they are entirely independent of one another because to function together would make too much sense and, in our world, the two are not made for such congruent union. Therefore, I felt forced to act out the words lest my mind should implode. Or, am I forced to speak out because mine own words are but simple therapy to myself? Who is to say? All I know is this and this for a certainty-this night would be his last and I would let him seduce me and I would ardently play my part. But, when the show ended and the curtain had closed and it was time for the player's to come out and take their bow, I would be the only one in this final scene to do so.

His timeless beauty held me in ways that only the stars could. He radiated so brightly that the blanket of darkness that long shrouded my body disappeared to a galaxy far from and unfamiliar to my senses. He shone an astral light from his dark, steely eyes that were not just beauty celestial but curiously more alien of neither doubt nor fear. As I imagined our two bodies furiously ascending and descending to planes beyond my experience, I felt an immense gravitational collapse that told me I was his no matter the distance of time or of space continuum. If he felt the same way about me it wasn't his words that convinced me for he never uttered a thing, nor did the faintest sound eject from his lips; instead, he seemed to just revolve around me and, in his slow spinning, I felt my own earth slowly rotate around his. The space that should have separated us before was now just a thin layer of ozone that couldn't even begin to contain us because like his close neighbor the moon, the more he waxed the less I waned...

It was in that moment of wistful fantasy that his class ended and my professor called out to me and asked me to stay for a moment longer while the rest of the class was dismissed.

"Absolute fidelity is a thing all men and women seek in their partners, but this a fool's wish, for neither he nor she can no more expect this of themselves' this trait than they can make demand upon others of the same type devotion. It unfair, unjust and not reasonable because what compels people to be dishonest is embedded firmly and early in our childhood years when we begin to..."

As she listened to her professor speak, his words seemed to drift off and become unintelligible to her. She was more occupied with his beauty than his words yet it was his words that made him so beautiful. Shaking her head from side to side, she hoped to sort out the conundrum that circled and bounced dizzyingly around inside her head. To somewhat assuage what might of made her palms sweat and her face blush even more profusely, she decided to completely tune out the rest of the lecture and put her head upon her desk and in that way she hoped she wouldn't continue to stare at him so sheepishly. But like most things that are forbidden and like most things that are self-destructive, her mind continued to pull and tempt her as even her eyes, allied thus to her brain, thought more thoroughly to betray her. Slowly raising her head and damning herself for her weakness, she cast up her grey eyes upon him and conjured up an image that would leave a birthmark upon her mind and a beauty mark upon her soul.

As the last rays of sunlight filtered through the narrow mullioned window, the light seemed to cast a supernatural glow over his purloined shadow. Radiant he shone in a simple white tee shirt and faded jeans with a brown thick leather belt and a polished, over-sized buckle. He was cavalier in ways that men aren't today. He was in his early forties, with dark hair, eyebrows, and a beard that just began to show the early signs of greying. There was steel in his eye and scorn on his lips, which curled like those of lion that need not roar out loudly, if at all, because you knew a lion when you saw one. His straight nose and prominent chin indicated a strong will which belied his gentler manner and his face, dashingly handsome, displayed a brutal, frightening candor that she knew was immune to lies, tricks, or treason.

She owned only one pair of jeans and she wore them all the time. If you were to walk next to her and take notice of her, you could recognize this by her disheveled hair and worn-out heels that these were still newer, fresher, and more durable in comparison. They fitted her well and the strong blue shade still seemed to retain its original color. They were heavily stitched with white thread that traveled down her leg like a track of railroad that connected seamlessly down to her full hips and long, slender legs to ankles that were narrow and elegant. And if you continued to look at her long enough you sensed by her steady, determined gait that she was not so much in a hurry to go somewhere but more in a hurry to speed away from what might be following her. When she did slow down, it was only to stop for a cup of coffee which steamed with heat and made small white puffs that wispily escaped the cup into the crisp, frigid air each time after she carefully took a sip. It was in these almost motionless moments that the locomotive of her heart came to a halfway stop and seemed to open and to empty the passengers that clung desperately to the depot of her innards: "envy" got off first because He was too important to be judged by the others..."hate" stepped off second because She was restless and didn't like to be in one place for too long...."narcissism" scampered off third because She was charmed by Her own reflection and needed more light to better see Herself..... "pride" was fourth to exit and only in this spot because He tripped over Himself when He tried over-hastily to go first.... "betrayal" came last as He trailed discreetly after all the others so He could see each wayfarer better before He decided who He could most easily take advantage of and whom He might be least detected by when He decided to partner up.

As she started to move again you could adjudge that she moved less quickly. One would have thought that after the emptying of her baggage she would be lighter and less encumbered, but ironically, this was wasn't the case at all. She seemed weary, downtrodden even, as if many more rugged miles lie ahead her. What earlier appeared like righteous determination toward a destination now seemed to have been derailed and gone unceremoniously off track. It was in that moment I decided to intervene and I waved her down emphatically like a commuter signaling that they were late for the departure and could not, under any circumstance, afford to miss their transport. As I hurriedly approached her she turned to face me with grey eyes and amber hair. Neither of us said a word as we each instinctively took one another's hand and the immediate intimacy

I felt was far greater than any lovemaking because to hold hands comfortably and serenely is more the measure of love than most anything between two people. In silence we regarded one another for what seemed an eternity. Then she spoke softly but confidently to me these words, "You think you know me, but you can't because I hardly even know myself. But this is what I do know: If you think you can seduce me don't because I am more skilled at that than any man, including you. I am not property and you'll not mark me as such with neither money nor comforts. My intuition is my power and beyond measure when I decide to listen to it and I did listen to it because I am here now speaking to you. If you think to hurt me or lie to me that is your choice, it's been done before and, yet, here I still stand. And lastly, what you put in is almost always what you'll get out." With that she reached up slightly and kissed me on the lips and she smelled and tasted of vanilla and cinnamon. She must have seen in my eyes I loved her already because the air around us grew warmer and the railroad crossing guard to her soul opened up and she let me safely pass through.

She pulled the amber colored-treated hair back from her soft grey eyes and then gently smiled into her vanity mirror and carefully plucked off just one side of her false eye lashes that she had worn the night before. She left it this way without touching the other one and thought to herself: this is how a fallen angel must feel with only one wing left to guide her.

As she arose from her cushioned seat, she readjusted her nightgown to cover the fullness of her breasts that spilled out from her. She was self-conscience of their large size and knew men looked there upon her before anywhere else. It's not that she wasn't beautiful no, on the contrary, it's just that she sadly always recalled at these times those words her deceased mother had told her when she was a young girl, "remember, my love life, the most dangerous part of any road is always the one with the most curves!"

Back then she had no idea what her mother had meant but now, since she was a woman, she understood clearly the wisdom and subtle warning of her words. Of course this didn't stop her from putting implants in the week following her mother's death—in fact looking back, I put these in precisely because you didn't want me to and you left me mother too young and too fragile. I did it because they made me feel sexy and I especially did it because I looked damned good in my dresses and because of the way they filled them out! Nothing as so simple as to attract a man, mother, as you had scolded me when I spoke to you of possibly having the procedure—that was too easy and men are very easily enticed, I responded—I did it for me, mother, and me alone.

She let the lingerie fall to the ground at that moment and reached up to her head with both hands and carefully unclipped the extensions she had attached to her hair. Without them her hair fell just above her shoulders and lacked the density and length the extensions had given her and, as she looked at herself once more into the mirror, it occurred to her that she somehow seemed less feminine.

Sitting back down she began to remove the make-up from her face. It was a slow process and one she always agonized over. She never really knew the right amount to put on and never really knew what colors suited her best and when she wore too much her mother would playfully poke at her and say, "you've got your war paint on thick tonight, my love life, those cowboys don't stand a chance!"

We would both have a good, quick laugh at this and then she would kiss me on the cheek before I walked out the door and into the night. I would always turn back to her before she closed the door and tell her that I loved her and she would always look at me and say, "one day you will be more like me than you ever could ever have imagined and you will say the same things to your daughter. You just wait and see; it is the way of things."

Her heart had been creased and turned back at the edge of the page like a bookmark that reminded her of where she was in her story. She preferred the touch, smell, and feel of books and not the online sort because she was tactile and when she marked her page it showed visually her progress and this seemed a small accomplishment no matter how far along she was or was not. She was a bit discolored from her age and a bit tattered from her travels, but what she held within those pages was her wisdom and her truths and this made her feel beautiful. She was quick to share the story of her book with others and even quicker to realize that what she shared with others that they had in many ways experienced the same types of things, too: painful things mostly, adorned with tragedy and decorated in silent suffering-for what can come from the terrible treatment to us by a person that should of cared for us can be a gift waiting to be given and unwrapped by the next person down our line that helps to break the cycle of abuse and neglect. In these moments it was when she thought most of the weight of her circumstances and felt the briefest of self-pity for herself, but this feeling was quickly effaced because she was certain that somebody in the world had it worse off than herself or, at least, that's what her few friends told her. Oddly enough she thought, too, of Einstein and always wondered out loud if this was what he meant by his theory of relativity? She doubted it in many ways, but it made sense to her in her own mind which caused her to giggle at the absurdity of the comparison. And then, in a flash, it came to her: all pain is relative and what is not and what can be universally objective is our loneliness! It was at this part in her book she always stopped to read and it was in this part her crease was always left intact. One day she hoped to give her book away and she longed for a partner to help her turn the page; she was certain he was out there and even more certain that he was looking for a great book to read.

It seems the more we worry about our future the more the mistakes in our past have a grasp of us. If we ever hope to escape history's clutch, we must stand firmly in the present wholly cognizant of ourselves, then inhale and exhale very deeply and assuredly bringing to mind calm existence, a one that lies down naturally like the moss over the solitary stone.

I'd reckon that most of our hurt in our lives comes through relationships, so it stands to reason that healing comes from the very same source. Looking back there is most likely a lot we would have done differently in response to our pain that it is very usually laced with much regret and what-was-I-thinking moments of terrible realization. But what I find more astounding is that in every love we've ever had, there was a moment in each that the world stopped on its axis, then begin to spin unnaturally again the other way, and for the briefest of moments we felt how God must always feel because the rarest gift He gives us is a reason to love yet again. Have faith. Believe in prayer.

I am frozen. Too afraid to move forward and too alone to look back. So I sit solid in place, waiting for something or someone to thaw me out. I am the feeling you get when you watch your dog slowly dying and just like the painful choice you have to make to send him beyond his suffering. I am the feeling you get like that child we all know who is forced to idle in the "Purgatory of no choice" living with only one parent because divorce became a better, more suitable solution for them. I am the feeling you get when the phone rings at an hour that only brings terrible news. I am the feeling you get when you have no more feeling to give. I am feeling you get when what you had is now all gone. I am the feeling. I am the get. I am the frozen.

I am a cloud...I am floating with not enough sun to dissipate me nor enough rain to sustain me. So I float...never really touching down but always hovering over things just beyond my reach...I sometimes cast a shadow and I sometimes extend my shade...I am a cloud...you can see me and I can see you...When you see me I can take the form of anything you can imagine in your mind: a bird, a dragon, an angel, a God...But, when I look down upon you, I see myself just like you but just out of touch and just beyond my grasp...Distance and, therefore, time separates us just as assuredly as our yearning does co-join us and, just as you long to be up here, I long to be down there...I am a cloud.

Did I dream this?

A mother's son was on the ground drowning in a pool of his own blood when from nowhere came up a man to help by trying to staunch the bleeding and give him CPR...as the man laid there looking up at his rescuer, the dying man spoke these words with tears and a soft, bright glow in his eyes:

"I have a mother whose husband she left because he beat her and told her lies. I hope she finds a man just like you that will rescue her and provide for her." He continued but with less energy as the blood flowed out of him even more freely. "I also have two younger sisters that never complain even though they barely have nice clothes to wear to school or more than one pair of shoes each between them. I hope my little sisters meet a man like you to marry when they get older because I am certain you will always do what you can to take care of their needs." As the man's breathing grew more labored and his face turned even paler, he forced out these last words to the kind stranger: "I never had a father who taught me anything, mostly because he was not around much. When I was smaller I wished and prayed every night to myself to have a man and father like you in my life." With these final words his life left him and the mysterious stranger who had

gently cradled his head the entire time, let out a
deep sigh and, finally, he quietly spoke these words
into the dead man's ear: "My Son I have always been
by your mother's side, your sisters' side, and by your
side for I am God almighty and the each of you live
eternally through my Word and in this world you
shall surely perish but you shall live everlasting up
above in Mine name and in Mine glory.

Quiver of Eros

What kind of ship did I build to wreck?

So distant heart made of sun setting speck.

Built laden of oak does salted moisture neglect.

Infinite ocean like darkened sky nearer mortality we respect.

Fore and aft call to darkened quarters

eternal mind too restless do reject.

Ego lain bare as the sun's rays will burn limitless yet conversely introspect.

A sirens call we but only men to rock, to death, none other outcome but to expect.

That's right. We never get everything we want and if we did, what beauty could be left to the things and persons we are finally blessed with? God is ineffable—His plan is eternal and no mortal can bear witness to it before the time it has arrived to us and across our path. That is why we have faith and that is why we endure in our belief in Him and in all of His creations.

Quiver of Eros

Nick Anthony Russo

About The Author

After a very successful career in business, Nick Anthony Russo decided to walk away from it all and pursue something he always had a true passion for, writing. This is his first book.

Made in the USA
Columbia, SC
27 November 2017